MERCURY

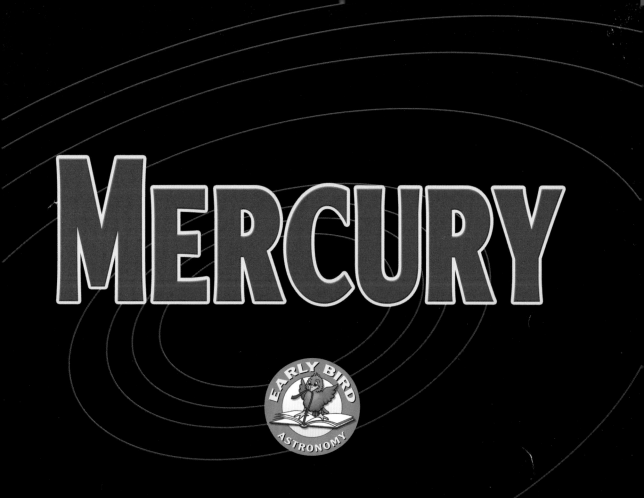

BY GREGORY L. VOGT

LERNER PUBLICATIONS COMPANY • MINNEAPOLIS

The images in this book are used with the permission of: © Dennis Hallinan/Alamy, p. 4;
© Christian Darkin/Photo Researchers, Inc., p. 5; © Science Source/Photo Researchers, Inc.,
pp. 6, 23, 35, 39, 40; © Joe Sohm/Visions of America, LLC/Alamy, p. 7; NASA/Johns Hopkins
University Applied Physics Laboratory/Carnegie Institution of Washington, pp. 8, 22, 27, 28,
31 (bottom), 32, 41 (bottom); © Frank Zullo/Photo Researchers, Inc., p. 9; AP Photo/Doug
Murray, p. 10; © Jaime Abecasis/SuperStock, p. 11; © Laura Westlund/Independent Picture
Service, pp. 12–13, 16, 19, 25; The International Astronomical Union/Martin Kommesser,
p. 14; NASA/JPL, pp. 15, 33, 37, 41 (top); © Peter Dawson/UpperCut Images/Getty Images,
p. 17; © Atlas Photo Bank/Photo Researchers, Inc., pp. 18, 46; © Antonio M. Rosario/Riser/
Getty Images, p. 20; © John R. Foster/Photo Researchers, Inc., p. 21; NASA/JPL/USGS, p. 24;
© Mauritius/SuperStock, p. 26; © Ron Miller, pp. 29, 42; NASA/Johns Hopkins University
Applied Physics Laboratory/Carnegie Institution of Washington/Brown University, p. 30;
NASA/Johns Hopkins University Applied Physics Laboratory/Arizona State University/Carnegie
Institution of Washington. Image reproduced courtesy of Science/AAAS, p. 31 (top); © D'Arco
Editori/De Agostini Picture Library/Getty Images, p. 34; ©MPI/Hulton Archive/Getty Images,
p. 36; © Matt Stroshane/Getty Images, p. 38; © Friedrich Saurer/Alamy, p. 43; © Chris Butler/
Photo Researchers, Inc., p. 47; © StockTrek/Photodisc/Getty Images, p. 48 (top); © John
Chumack/Photo Researchers, Inc., p. 48 (bottom).

Front Cover: NASA/Johns Hopkins University Applied Physics Laboratory/Carnegie Institution
of Washington.

Lerner Publications Company
A division of Lerner Publishing Group, Inc.
241 First Avenue North
Minneapolis, MN 55401 U.S.A.

Website address: www.lernerbooks.com

Library of Congress Cataloging-in-Publication Data

Vogt, Gregory.
    Mercury / by Gregory L. Vogt.
        p.   cm. — (Early bird astronomy)
    Includes index.
    ISBN 978–0–7613–4150–5 (lib. bdg. : alk. paper)
    1. Mercury (Planet)—Juvenile literature. I. Title.
QB611.V644 2010
523.41—dc22   2008032826

Manufactured in the United States of America
1 2 3 4 5 6 – BP – 15 14 13 12 11 10

CONTENTS

Be a Word Detective 5

Chapter 1
CLOSEST TO THE SUN 6

Chapter 2
MERCURY'S NEIGHBORHOOD 12

Chapter 3
MERCURY UP CLOSE 21

Chapter 4
THE CALORIS BASIN 29

Chapter 5
VISIT TO A SMALL PLANET 35

A Note to Adults on Sharing a Book 44

Learn More about Mercury 45

Glossary 46

Index 47

BE A WORD DETECTIVE

Can you find these words as you read about Mercury? Be a detective and try to figure out what they mean. You can turn to the glossary on page 46 for help.

asteroids

astronomers

atmosphere

axis

comets

core

craters

elliptical

gravity

meteorites

orbit

quake

rotates

solar system

spacecraft

telescope

CHAPTER 1
CLOSEST TO THE SUN

Just before dawn, a tiny dot glows in the sky.
It is the planet Mercury. Mercury is the Sun's
smallest planet. It is also the planet closest to

We can watch some of the planets in the night sky. A telescope (TEL-luh-skohp) can help us get a better view. A telescope makes faraway objects look bigger and closer. But Mercury is harder to see. It is often lost in the Sun's glare. You have to know just where and when to look for it.

Scientists have to use special equipment (LEFT) when looking toward the Sun and Mercury. Without special filters, the Sun's glare would hurt the scientists' eyes.

Sometimes Mercury is behind the Sun and can't be seen at all. Sometimes it is in front of the Sun. It can't be seen then without special equipment. The Sun is too bright. At other times, Mercury is to the right or left of the Sun. That's when people can see it with just their eyes.

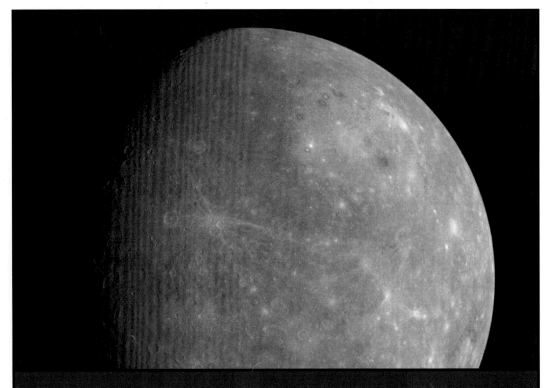

Mercury is a small planet very close to the Sun. Often the Sun's glare keeps us from seeing Mercury from Earth.

Mercury can be seen in the sky just before dawn. (THE PLANET APPEARS NEAR THE CENTER OF THE PHOTO.) Often the best time to see Mercury in our sky is a few minutes before the Sun rises.

From Earth, Mercury looks like a tiny, faint star. To see it at all, you may have to get up before sunrise. In the morning, Mercury rises in the east just before the Sun does. It can be seen only for a few minutes. Then Mercury fades in the daylight.

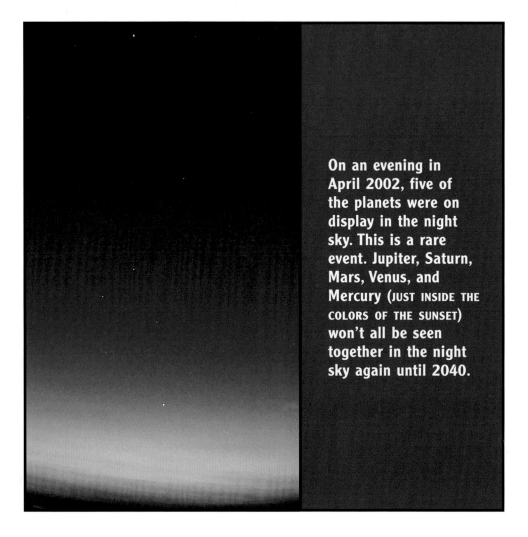

On an evening in April 2002, five of the planets were on display in the night sky. This is a rare event. Jupiter, Saturn, Mars, Venus, and Mercury (JUST INSIDE THE COLORS OF THE SUNSET) won't all be seen together in the night sky again until 2040.

About a month and a half later, Mercury will show up on the other side of the Sun. This time, it can be seen in the western sky just after sunset. Mercury sinks out of sight a few minutes after the Sun sets.

People have been looking at Mercury since ancient times. Long ago, the Romans lived in Italy. They believed in many gods. The ancient Romans named the planet Mercury after one of their gods.

In ancient Roman stories, the god Mercury brought messages to the other gods. He had wings on his feet and could fly very fast through the air.

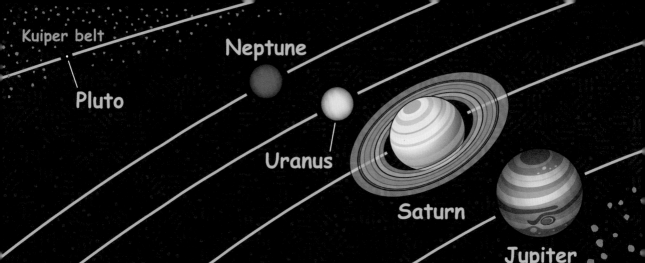

Kuiper belt

Neptune

Pluto

Uranus

Saturn

Jupiter

CHAPTER 2
MERCURY'S NEIGHBORHOOD

Mercury and Earth share the same neighborhood in space. They are both a part of the solar system. The solar system includes the Sun and eight planets. Dwarf planets, asteroids (A-stur-oydz), and other objects are also a part of the solar system. Dwarf planets are smaller than the eight main planets.

This diagram shows planets and objects in our solar system. The asteroid belt and Kuiper belt are groups of rocky and icy objects.

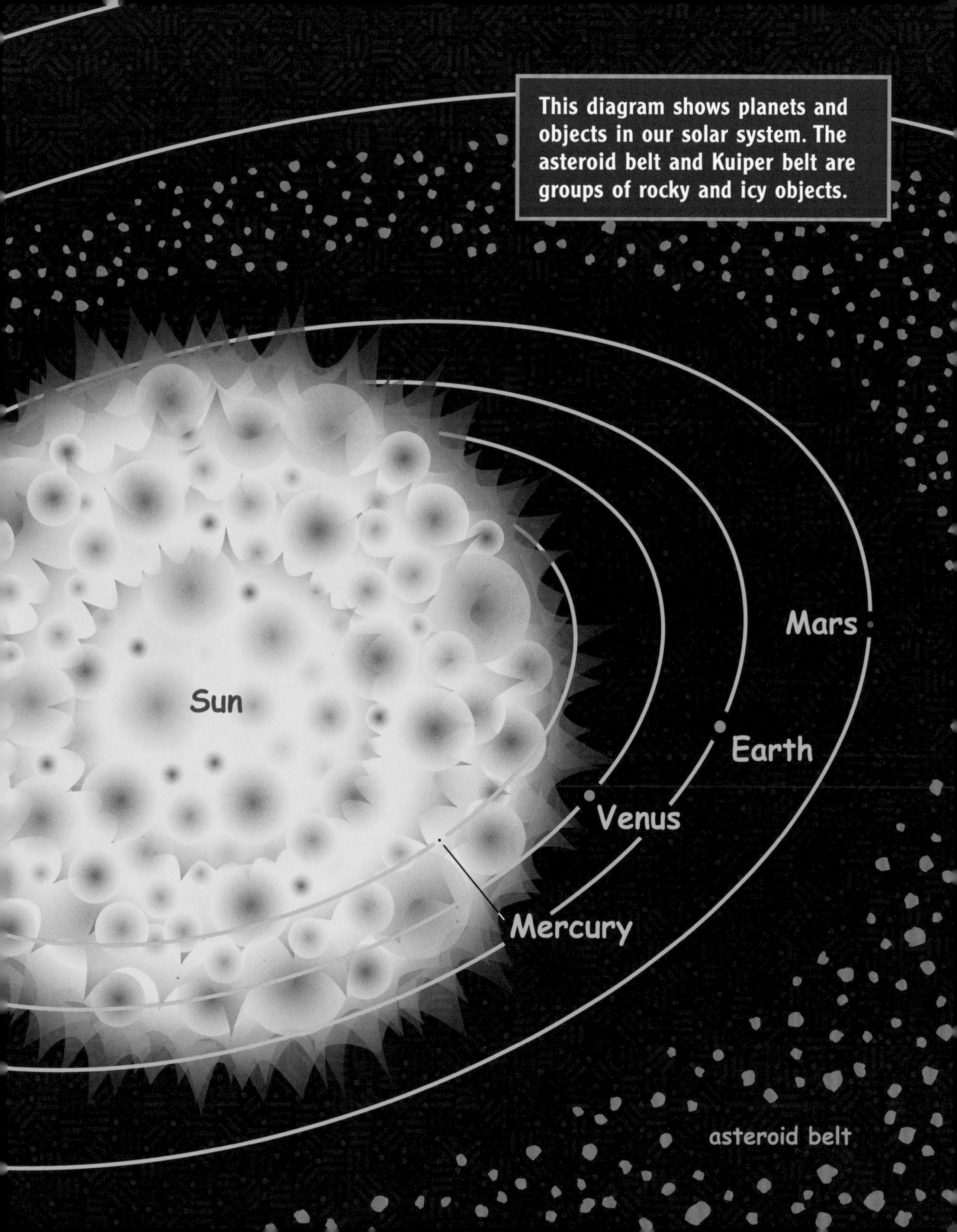

Mars

Earth

Venus

Sun

Mercury

asteroid belt

The Sun lies at the center of the solar system. Each planet is a different distance from the Sun. The planets closest to the Sun are Mercury, Venus, Earth, and Mars. These four planets are mostly made of solid rock. Scientists call them the rocky planets.

This picture shows the eight planets in our solar system. The Sun appears on the left, and the dwarf planet Pluto is on the right. This picture shows the size of each planet compared to others.

Neptune, Uranus, Saturn, and Jupiter (LEFT TO RIGHT) are gas planets. They are much larger than the rocky planets.

Jupiter, Saturn, Uranus, and Neptune are called gas giants. They are mostly made of gas. They are the largest planets in the solar system and the farthest from Earth.

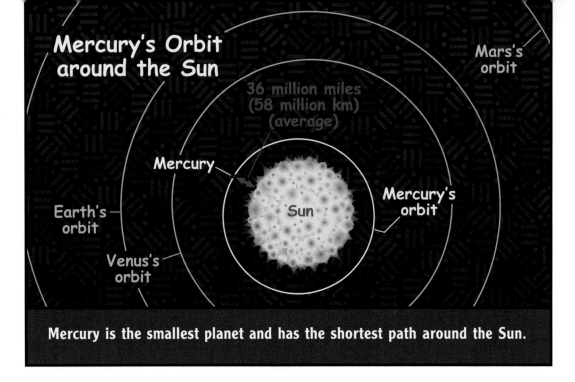

Mercury's Orbit
around the Sun

Mars's
orbit

36 million miles
(58 million km)
(average)

Mercury

Sun

Mercury's
orbit

Earth's
orbit

Venus's
orbit

Mercury is the smallest planet and has the shortest path around the Sun.

Mercury is only 3,000 miles (4,900 kilometers) across. Earth is about two and a half times larger than Mercury. The largest planet, Jupiter, is 29 times larger than Mercury.

Mercury follows a path around the Sun. That path is called an orbit. It takes 88 Earth days for Mercury to make one orbit around the Sun. That's the shortest trip around the Sun for any planet. Earth takes about 365 days to orbit once.

Mercury orbits the Sun at 30 miles (48 km) per second. That's 107,000 miles (172,000 km) per hour. Imagine you had a car that could go that fast. You could drive from New York to Los Angeles in just 93 seconds.

Imagine driving a car so fast that you could cross the United States in just over a minute and a half. That is how fast Mercury orbits around the Sun.

Mercury's distance from the Sun changes as it orbits.

Mercury's orbit around the Sun does not form a perfect circle. The orbit is shaped more like an egg. Scientists call this shape elliptical (ih-LIHP-tih-cuhl).

Mercury's elliptical orbit means that the planet sometimes travels close to the Sun. And sometimes it is farther away. Mercury is 29 million miles (47 million km) from the Sun at the closest point in its orbit. It is 43 million miles (70 million km) at its farthest point.

Mercury rotates (ROH-tayts) as it orbits. To rotate is to spin around like a toy top. Mercury spins around an imaginary line called an axis (AK-suhs). The axis runs through the planet from Mercury's north pole to its south pole.

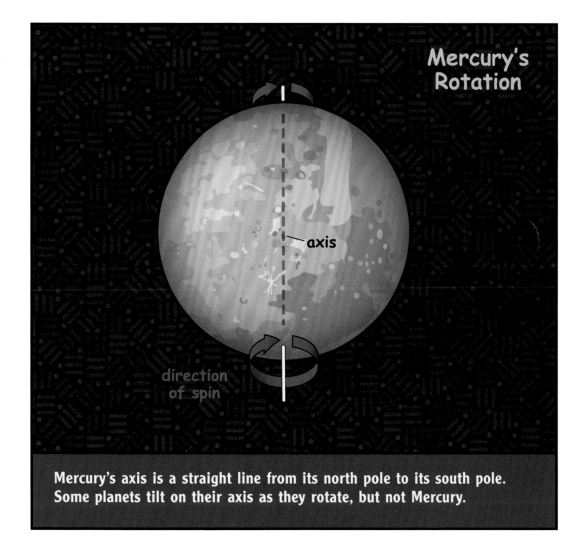

Mercury's Rotation

axis

direction of spin

Mercury's axis is a straight line from its north pole to its south pole. Some planets tilt on their axis as they rotate, but not Mercury.

Earth takes 24 hours to rotate all the way around. But Mercury takes 1,408 hours to rotate once. As a planet rotates, one side faces the Sun. It is daytime on that side. One side faces away from the Sun. It is night on that side. Both days and nights last for a long time on Mercury.

One side of Mercury is in shadow as it travels around the Sun.

This illustration shows what the Sun would look like from Mercury's surface. Is Mercury hot during the day?

CHAPTER 3
MERCURY
UP CLOSE

Mercury is one of the hottest planets. It is also one of the coldest planets. Daytime temperatures on Mercury reach more than 800°F (430°C). That's about twice as hot as an oven needs to be to bake a pizza.

While one side of Mercury bakes in sunlight, the other side is dark. It is very cold on the dark side with no sun to warm it. The temperature on the dark side drops to –280°F (–170°C).

Sunlight warms one side of Mercury (RIGHT). The side away from the Sun (LEFT) stays cold.

In this photograph, Mercury looks like a small black dot as it passes in front of the Sun.

Mercury has a very thin atmosphere (AT-muhs-feer). An atmosphere is a layer of gases around a planet. A planet has to have gravity to have an atmosphere. Gravity is a force that pulls two objects toward each other. Mercury's gravity is weak. It cannot hold onto its atmosphere.

A planet also has to be cool to have an atmosphere. If a planet is too hot, the gases get hot too. Then they blow away. The Sun's heat has driven off almost all Mercury's gases.

Earth has a large moon (ABOVE) that orbits our planet. Mercury has no moons.

Most of the other planets in the solar system have moons. Earth, Mars, and Jupiter have moons. So does Saturn, Uranus, Neptune, and the dwarf planet Pluto. Jupiter, Saturn, Uranus, and Neptune also have rings. But Mercury has no moons and no rings.

The surface of Mercury is completely covered with dark colored rock. Mercury has a core of iron. A core is a ball of metal or rock at the center of a planet. Mercury's core is very large. It is 2,237 miles (3,600 km) across.

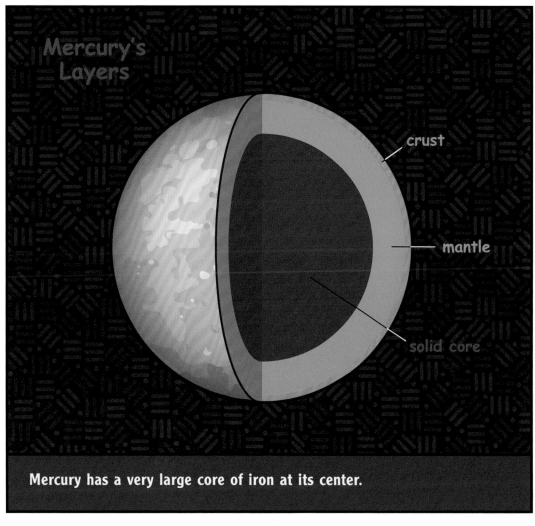

Mercury's Layers

crust

mantle

solid core

Mercury has a very large core of iron at its center.

If you gave Mercury a quick look, you might mistake it for the Moon. Like the Moon, Mercury has many smooth areas called plains. It also has many craters. Craters are bowl-shaped holes.

This photo shows Mercury's surface covered with craters. Look at the photo of Earth's Moon on page 24. The surfaces of Mercury and the Moon look very similar.

This close-up photo of Mercury's surface shows the many craters that dot the planet.

Most craters are formed when meteorites (MEE-tee-uh-ryets) slam into a planet or a moon. Meteorites are pieces of space rock or metal. Each time a meteorite hits Mercury, it leaves a crater. Meteorites come in many sizes, so Mercury's craters come in many sizes.

Mercury has many large cliffs. The cliffs were formed by cracks in Mercury's surface. Mercury began as a ball of melted rock and metal. As the planet cooled, its surface hardened. Mercury shrank and cracked. In many places, one side of a crack rose higher than the other side. That shifting formed Mercury's cliffs.

This image of Mercury's surface shows the cliffs that are seen all over the planet.

This illustration shows a very large space rock hitting Mercury. What are very large space rocks called?

CHAPTER 4
THE CALORIS BASIN

Asteroids are space rocks that can be hundreds of miles across. Asteroids are smaller than planets. But they are larger than meteorites. About four billion years ago, a large asteroid crashed into Mercury.

This asteroid left a crater 800 miles (1,300 km) wide on Mercury. The crater is about the size of the state of Texas. Scientists named the giant crater the Caloris Basin (KUH-lawr-ihs BAY-suhn).

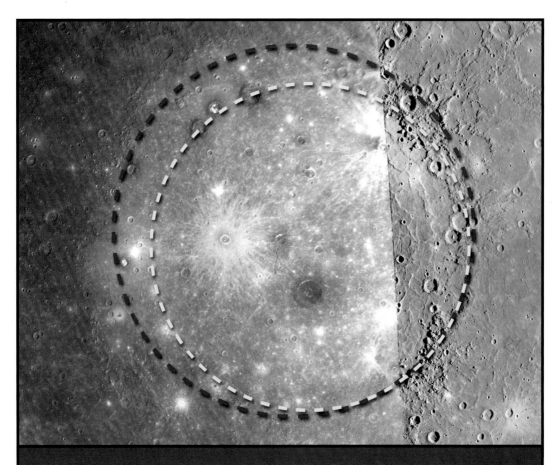

This image puts together two photos of the Caloris Basin taken in different years. At first, scientists thought the basin covered the area shown by the yellow dotted line. But the second photo showed that the basin was larger (SHOWN BY THE BLUE DOTTED LINE).

TOP: This image was specially colored to show details of Mercury's surface. The pale orange circle in the middle shows where the Caloris asteroid hit.
BOTTOM: This image shows two of the biggest craters in the Caloris Basin. They are at the bottom of the photo, surrounded by dark rings.

The Caloris Basin is surrounded by mountains. Some of the mountains are almost 2 miles (3 km) high. These are the highest mountains on Mercury.

Cracks stretch out in straight lines from a crater in the center of the Caloris Basin.

In the center of the basin is a smaller crater. Cracks in the planet's surface spread outward from this crater. From above, the cracks look like thin legs spreading out from a round body. Scientists have nicknamed this feature the Spider.

Scientists think the Caloris asteroid smashed into pieces when it hit Mercury. It also smashed the rock on the planet's surface. Pieces of rock flew into the air in a huge umbrella shape. The land around the asteroid was pushed upward to form the mountains. Heat made by the blast melted the rock in the center of the basin.

All these craters and ridges make up a part of the Caloris Basin.

The Caloris asteroid also caused a strong quake. The motion of the quake spread out in waves across the planet's surface. In just a few minutes, the waves all crashed together on the opposite side of Mercury. That crash shook and tumbled the rock there. The bumpy rock can still be seen on that side of the planet.

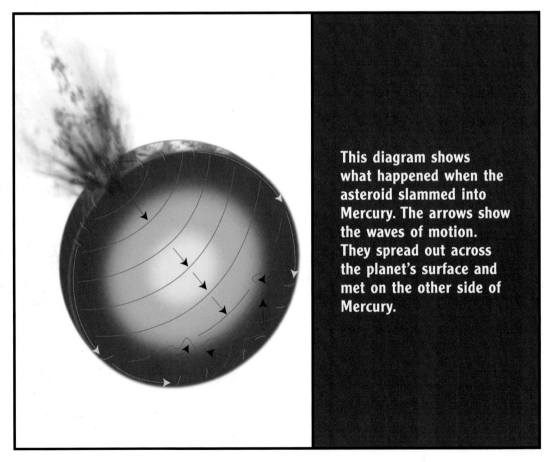

This diagram shows what happened when the asteroid slammed into Mercury. The arrows show the waves of motion. They spread out across the planet's surface and met on the other side of Mercury.

Scientists use this equipment to track Mercury. What do we call scientists who study the planets?

CHAPTER 5
VISIT TO A SMALL PLANET

Only two spacecraft have ever visited Mercury. The first was *Mariner 10*. The United States launched *Mariner 10* in 1973. There were no humans aboard the spacecraft.

Mariner 10 was sent toward the Sun. It passed the planet Venus. Then it passed by Mercury. It took photographs of the planets as it passed.

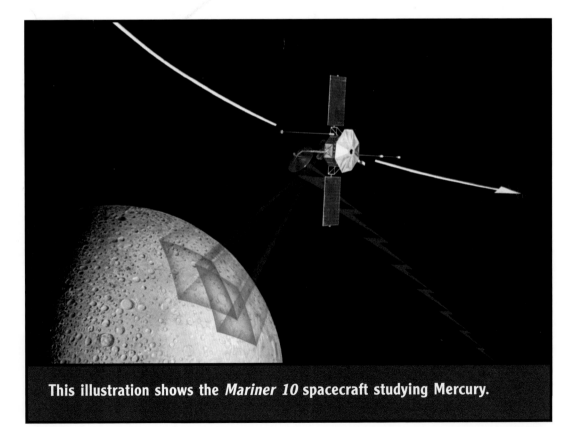

This illustration shows the *Mariner 10* spacecraft studying Mercury.

Mariner 10 took this photo of the side of Mercury facing the Sun. The spacecraft passed by Mercury in 1973 and 1974.

Mariner 10 swung around the Sun and passed Mercury again. It made one more pass in 1974. Then *Mariner 10* ran out of fuel and was shut down. The *Mariner 10* pictures only showed about one-third of Mercury's surface.

The *Messenger* spacecraft was launched in 2004. A rocket (ABOVE) carried *Messenger* into space.

Messenger is the second spacecraft to explore Mercury. It was launched by the United States in 2004. *Messenger* is expected to orbit Mercury in 2011. It has already passed near Mercury and has taken more pictures. The pictures show new parts of Mercury's surface.

By 2019, another spacecraft is expected to arrive at Mercury. This one is being built by the European Space Agency. The spacecraft is called *BepiColombo*.

The *BepiColombo* spacecraft is shown orbiting Mercury in this illustration. *BepiColombo* is named after Italian scientist Giuseppe (Bepi) Colombo, who helped the United States with *Mariner 10*.

Astronomers carefully study the pictures of Mercury's surface. One thing they are looking for is ice. How could ice be found on Mercury? It is too close to the Sun. But astronomers believe that Mercury may have a few spots the Sun doesn't reach. Mercury's north and south poles may have deep craters. The floors of the craters would always be in the shadows. If no sunlight reaches the crater floors, they would stay cold. They may even be covered in ice.

Mercury's cold north pole is shown in this image from *Messenger*. Scientists believe the craters on the poles could have ice in them.

Mercury's south pole (ABOVE) could also have ice. The ice might be found in the deep craters that dot the pole (RIGHT).

If there is ice on Mercury, where did it come from? Space objects might have brought ice to the planet. Comets are large ice balls that orbit the Sun. Comets could have struck Mercury and left ice behind. Or there might be water inside Mercury. The water could seep out and freeze in the craters.

This illustration shows a crater on one of Mercury's poles. The crater could contain ice.

A new kind of spacecraft will be needed to find the ice. The spacecraft will have to land on a polar crater floor. If there is ice, the spacecraft will send a signal to scientists on Earth.

The polar craters may also provide a place for human astronauts to land on Mercury. In the shadows, the astronauts would always be protected from the blazing Sun. These astronauts may discover many new things about the solar system's smallest planet.

In the future, astronauts might land on Mercury to study it further.

ON SHARING A BOOK

When you share a book with a child, you show that reading is important. To get the most out of the experience, read in a comfortable, quiet place. Turn off the television and limit other distractions, such as telephone calls. Be prepared to start slowly. Take turns reading parts of this book. Stop occasionally and discuss what you're reading. Talk about the photographs. If the child begins to lose interest, stop reading. When you pick up the book again, revisit the parts you have already read.

BE A VOCABULARY DETECTIVE

The word list on page 5 contains words that are important in understanding the topic of this book. Be word detectives and search for the words as you read the book together. Talk about what the words mean and how they are used in the sentence. Do any of these words have more than one meaning? You will find the words defined in a glossary on page 46.

WHAT ABOUT QUESTIONS?

Use questions to make sure the child understands the information in this book. Here are some suggestions:

What did this paragraph tell us? What does this picture show? What do you think we'll learn about next? Can we see Mercury from Earth? How long does it take Mercury to travel around the Sun? What is Mercury made of? Does Mercury have moons? How do scientists study Mercury?

If the child has questions, don't hesitate to respond with questions of your own, such as What do *you* think? Why? What is it that you don't know? If the child can't remember certain facts, turn to the index.

INTRODUCING THE INDEX

The index helps readers get information without searching throughout the whole book. Turn to the index on page 48. Choose an entry, such as *orbit*, and ask the child to use the index to find out how many moons Mercury has. Repeat with as many entries as you like. Ask the child to point out the differences between an index and a glossary. (The index helps readers find information quickly, while the glossary tells readers what words mean.)

MERCURY

BOOKS

Hoffman, Sara. *The Little Book of Space*. Minnetonka, MN: Two-Can, 2005. In this book, the author describes the planets of the solar system and different missions to space.

Lauw, Darlene, and Lim Cheng Puay. *Earth and the Solar System*. New York: Crabtree, 2002. Through activities and experiments, Lauw provides a hands-on understanding of our planet and the solar system.

WEBSITES

Extreme Space
http://solarsystem.nasa.gov/kids/index.cfm
The National Aeronautics and Space Administration (NASA) created this astronomy website just for kids.

Jet Propulsion Laboratory Photojournal
http://photojournal.jpl.nasa.gov/index.html
This NASA website contains thousands of great planet pictures.

Messenger
http://messenger.jhuapl.edu/why_mercury/index.html
Learn about *Messenger's* mission, view the image gallery, and catch the latest news on this NASA website.

NASA Science for Kids
http://nasascience.nasa.gov/kids
Readers will find lots of fun facts and activities about the solar system on this site.

The Space Place
http://spaceplace.nasa.gov/en/kids/
Go to this NASA Web page for activities, quizzes, and games all about outer space.

GLOSSARY

asteroids (A-stur-oydz): rocky bodies that travel through space around the Sun. Asteroids are smaller than planets but larger than meteorites.

astronomers (uh-STRAH-nuh-muhrz): scientists who study outer space

atmosphere (AT-muhs-feer): a layer of gases surrounding a planet or moon

axis (AK-suhs): an imaginary line that goes through a planet from top to bottom. A planet spins on its axis.

comets: large chunks of ice, dust, and rock that orbit the Sun

core: a large ball of rock or metal at the center of a planet

craters: bowl-shaped holes formed when a space rock or metal hits a planet or a moon

elliptical (ih-LIHP-tih-cuhl): oval shaped

gravity (GRA-vuh-tee): a force that pulls two objects toward each other

meteorites (MEE-tee-uh-ryets): pieces of space rock or metal

orbit: the path of a planet, moon, or other object in space around the Sun or a planet. *Orbit* can also mean to move along this path.

quake: the shaking of a planet's surface

rotates (ROH-tayts): spins around like a toy top

solar system: a group of planets and other objects that travel around the Sun

spacecraft: a machine that travels from Earth to outer space

telescope (TEL-luh-skohp): an instrument that makes faraway objects appear bigger and closer

INDEX

Pages listed in **bold** type refer to photographs.

asteroids, 12, **29**–31, 33, 34
atmosphere, 23

Caloris Basin, **30–31**, **32**–33
cliffs on Mercury, **28**
core of Mercury, **25**
craters on Mercury, **26–27**, 40, **42**

gases on Mercury, 23

ice on Mercury, 40–42

Mercury (Roman god), **11**
meteorites, 27
moons around Mercury, 24

orbit, **16**–17, 18

rotation, **19**–20

solar system, **12–13**, **14**–15
spacecraft, 35, **36**–37, **38–39**
Spider, the, **32**

telescope, **7**
temperature, 21–22